AMERICAN REVOLUTION FOR KIDS

US REVOLUTIONARY TIMELINES COLONIZATION TO ABOLITION

4TH GRADE CHILDREN'S AMERICAN REVOLUTION HISTORY

In this book, we're going to talk about the events that occurred in America from the first colonies through the American Revolution and the fight to end slavery. So, let's get right to it!

From the time that America was colonized by Europeans to the time when every American was considered to be a free citizen took over two hundred years. Here are some of the important events that led from the first colonial settlements to the abolitionist movement.

HAEC EST EFFIGIES LIGVRIS MIRANDA
RATE QVI PENETRAVIT IN .
COLVMBI ANTIPODVM
ORBEM · EST ·
CHRISTOPHER COLUMBUS

DISCOVERY OF THE AMERICAS AND THE COLONIZATION OF AMERICA

After Columbus set foot in America, it took over 90 years for Europeans to start coming to the new lands. At the beginning, these settlers were still ruled by the countries of the "Old World," such as England and Spain. Eventually, the settlers wanted their own country and that's when thoughts of revolution began to take hold.

1492
The Italian explorer Columbus "discovers" the Americas although he believes he has found a route to the Far East.

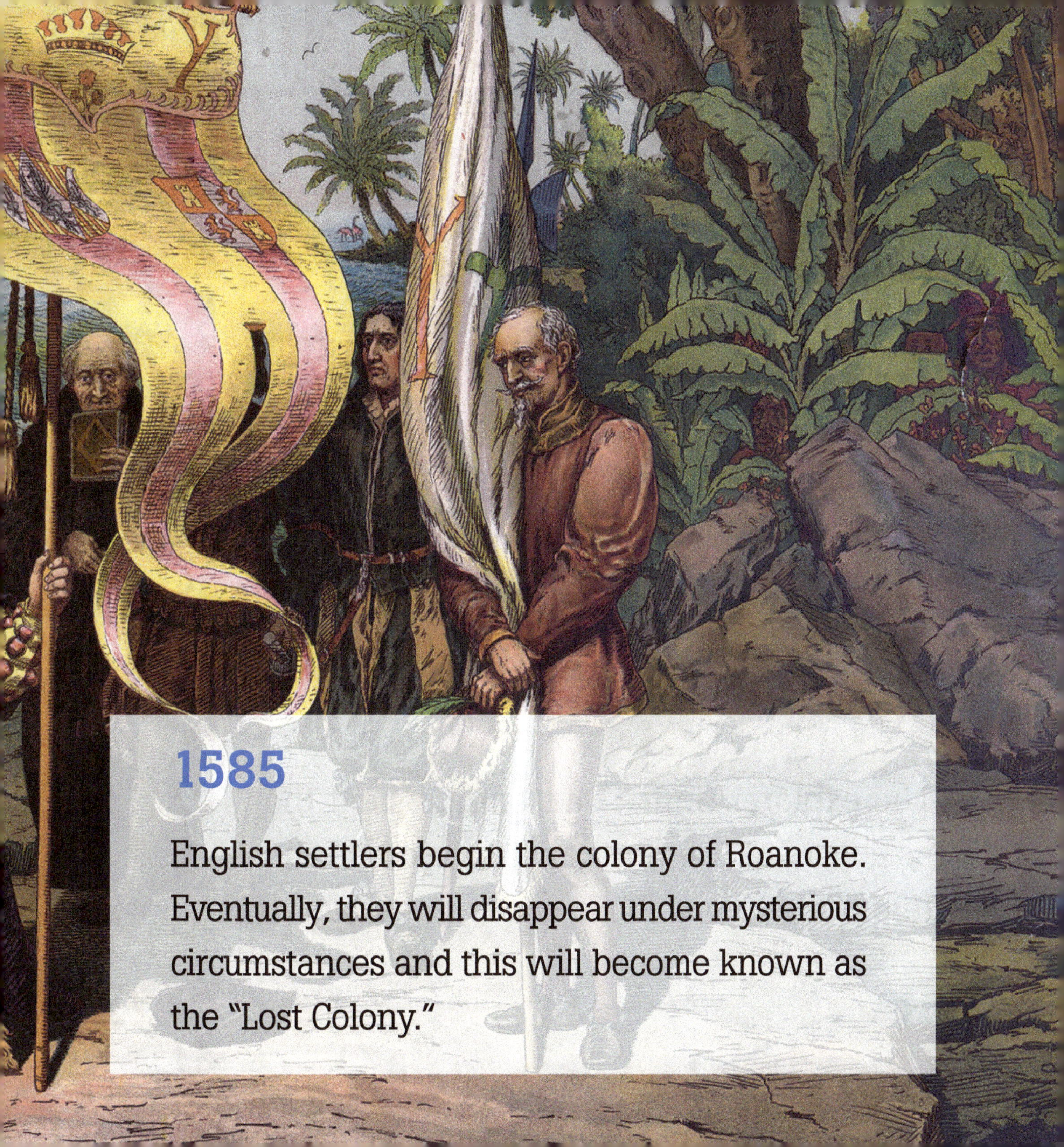

1585

English settlers begin the colony of Roanoke. Eventually, they will disappear under mysterious circumstances and this will become known as the "Lost Colony."

1607

The settlement of Jamestown is founded by English settlers.

1609

Only 60 settlers from Jamestown survive the winter of 1609 through 1610. It is described as the "starving time" because 440 settlers lose their lives.

1609

The explorer Henry Hudson maps out the coastline of the northeast as well as the Hudson River, which is named after him.

JAMESTOWN

WEDDING DAY OF JOHN ROLFE AND POCAHONTAS

1614

Tobacco farmer John Rolfe from Jamestown marries Pocahontas, the daughter of a Native American chief.

1614

The colony of New Netherland is founded by Dutch settlers.

1619

The first slaves brought from Africa come to the Jamestown settlement to work.

1619

The House of Burgesses, Virginia's first government of representatives, convenes at Jamestown.

1620

The Pilgrims establish a colony at Plymouth.

1626

The Dutch buy the island now known as Manhattan from the native tribe living there.

1629

A royal charter is drawn up for the colony that would become Massachusetts Bay.

1630

The settlement now known as the city of Boston is established by the Puritans.

1632

The colony of Maryland is begun by Lord Calvert.

1636

Providence Plantation is begun by Roger Williams after he is forced to leave Massachusetts for his religious views.

1637

The Pequot native people are almost wiped out during a war with settlers in Massachusetts.

BOSTON CITY HALL

1638

The colony of New Sweden is established close to the Delaware River.

1639

The government of the colony of Connecticut creates the first Constitution in America called the Fundamental Orders.

1655

The Dutch begin to rule in New Sweden.

1656

Settlers who describe themselves as Quakers come to New England.

1663

The Carolina province is founded.

1664

The English capture New Netherland from the Dutch and rename it New York province. The name of the settlement of New Amsterdam is changed to New York.

1670

In South Carolina, the city of Charlestown is established.

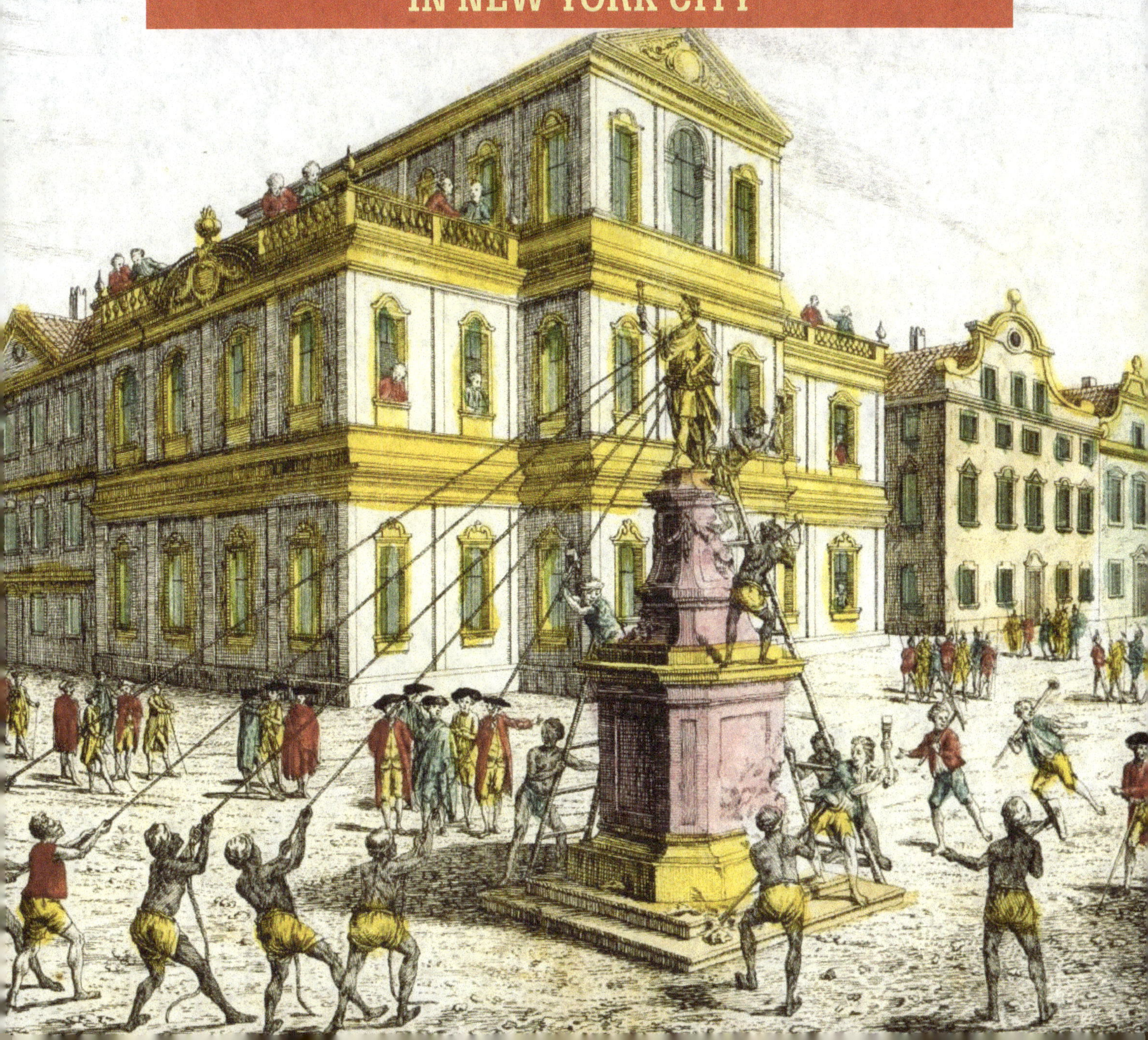

TOPPLING THE STATUE OF THE KING
IN NEW YORK CITY

1675

The New England colonists go to war with a group of tribes of Native Americans. The war is called King Philip's War. The Wampanoag people, who were once friends with the Pilgrims from Plymouth, are involved in the war.

1676

Nathaniel Bacon leads a group of settlers to fight against the governor of Virginia, William Berkeley. This event was later called Bacon's Rebellion.

1681

William Penn establishes the Pennsylvania province.

1682

The settlement of Philadelphia in Pennsylvania is founded.

1690

Spanish settlers begin taking over land in what is now Texas.

NATHANIEL BACON

FANCIFUL REPRESENTATION OF THE SALEM WITCH TRIAL

1692

Twenty people are accused and killed for supposedly practicing witchcraft in Salem, Massachusetts.

1699

The capital of the colony of Virginia is moved from the city of Jamestown to the city of Williamsburg.

1701

Delaware is split from the colony of Pennsylvania to become a separate colony.

1702

East Jersey and West Jersey are combined to form New Jersey, a new colony.

1702

Queen Anne's war is fought between England and France for control of the North American continent.

GEORGIA STATE CAPITOL, ATLANTA

1712

Carolina province is divided into North and South Carolina.

1718

New Orleans in Louisiana is established by the French.

1732

James Oglethorpe establishes the Georgia province.

1733

Settlers start coming to Georgia.

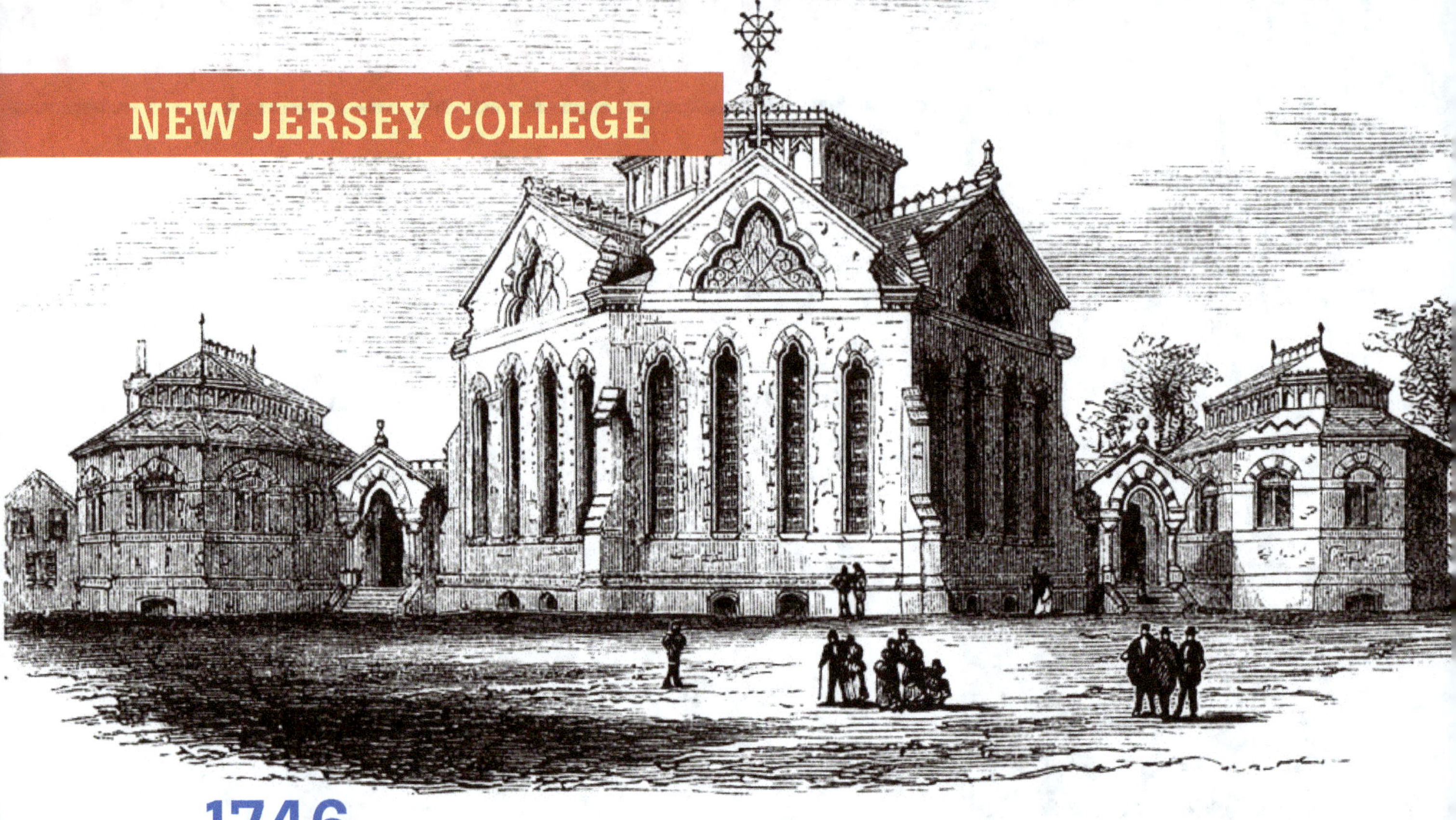

1746

Princeton University, which was originally called the College of New Jersey, is established.

1754

The French and Indian War starts. The British colonies are fighting the French. Both the colonists and the French align themselves with Native American tribes.

1763

The British are victorious in the French and Indian War and they gain more North American lands.

THE COLONIES WANT INDEPENDENCE

By 1765, the colonies had been established in America for over one hundred years. At the beginning, they wanted religious freedom but didn't resent the rule of their mother country of Great Britain. However, that changed when the British started to raise taxes. The American colonists began to want their own government and "no taxation without representation."

1765

The Stamp Act is passed by
the British. All public documents, such
as newspapers and contracts, were taxed.
This led to a great deal of tension between the
British and their colonies.

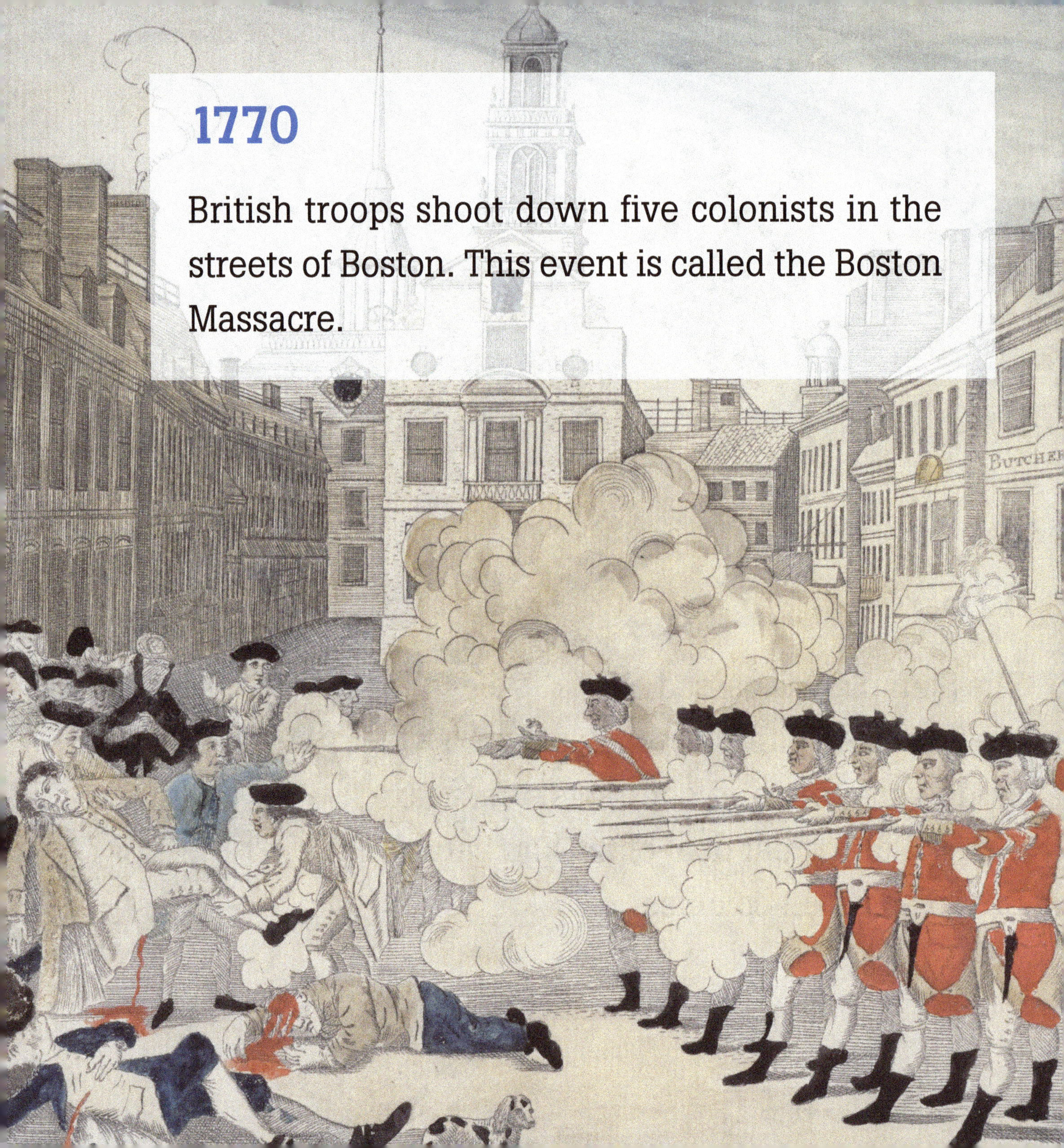

1770

British troops shoot down five colonists in the streets of Boston. This event is called the Boston Massacre.

1773

The Sons of Liberty, a group of colonists who want independence from the British, dump large amounts of tea into the harbor at Boston to protest British taxes on tea. The event is later called the Boston "Tea Party."

THE FIRST CONTINENTAL CONGRESS · 1774

1774

The First Continental Congress convenes in Philadelphia. Representatives from each of the colonies get together to unify against the British taxation.

THE REVOLUTIONARY WAR BREAKS OUT

The colonists have finally had enough. They decide that they will risk their lives to ensure that they have their own country.

1775

Paul Revere rides his horse to send a warning to the colonists that the "British are coming."

1775

The fighting begins at the Battle of Lexington and Concord. The Americans are victorious.

BATTLE OF LEXINGTON

1775

Fort Ticonderoga, which is held by the British, is captured by the Green Mountain Boys. Their leaders are Ethan Allen and the notorious Benedict Arnold, who eventually changed over to the British side.

1775

The Battle of Bunker Hill, one of the major battles of the war, is fought.

1776

The Declaration of Independence is drafted by Thomas Jefferson and other statesmen and approved by the Continental Congress.

1776

On Christmas night, George Washington and his men go across the Delaware River to make a surprise attack on the British.

1777

The design of the flag for the United States of America is chosen.

The Battles of Saratoga take place. The Americans are victorious and John Burgoyne, the British general, surrenders.

1777–1778

Washington gathers the soldiers of the Continental Army at Valley Forge, where they train and increase their efficiency as a fighting unit.

1778

France, ally to the new country, recognizes the United States as separate from Britain under the terms of the Treaty of Alliance.

1781

The Articles of Confederation are drafted. They specify details about how the United States will be governed.

1781

The last major battle of the Revolutionary War, the Battle of Yorktown, is a victory for the Americans.

1783

The Treaty of Paris is the official end of the war.

BATTLE OF YORKTOWN

THE ABOLITIONIST MOVEMENT BEGINS

Soon after the new country was established, there was a debate between North and South regarding whether landowners should be allowed to keep slaves. People in the North wanted to abolish slavery, but the economy of the South depended on the work of slaves. The women's movement that was pushing for women's rights also added reinforcement to the abolitionist movement.

1791

The Bill of Rights is drafted as an addition to the United States Constitution. It centers on the personal freedoms of United States citizens, but slaves and Native Americans are still not freed.

1861 to 1865

The Civil War is fought, primarily over the issue of slavery. The North wins and slaves are freed.

1863

President Lincoln places his signature on the Emancipation Proclamation, which states that the slaves in the South should be freed.

LIBERTY
TO ALL
PROCLAMATION

1865

The Thirteenth Amendment is passed. Slavery is finally abolished in the United States, but it would take many more years for African Americans to be treated equally. It would take until 1920 for women to be given voting rights and until 1924 for Native Americans to be given that right.

1868

The Fourteenth Amendment is approved. It guarantees
all citizens born in the United States full rights with
no discrimination based on race.

EFFECTS OF COLONIZATION

The British colonies were under the rule of Great Britain's monarchy for over 100 years. Then, because Britain needed money, they began to tax the colonies excessively. This taxation without appropriate representation led to ill

feelings and then to all out war. The Americans won against the British and the new country was called the United States of America. Eventually, the spirit of freedom led to the abolitionist movement and the freeing of slaves.

Awesome! Now that you've read about important events in America's history, you may want to read more about the American Revolution in the Baby Professor book US and British Military Leaders during the American Revolution.

Visit
BABY PROFESSOR
EDUCATION KIDS
www.BabyProfessorBooks.com
to download Free Baby Professor eBooks
and view our catalog of new and exciting
Children's Books